Life
BRIGHTENERS
for
Teens

H. Curtis & Karen McDaniel

WATERBROOK
PRESS

LIFE BRIGHTENERS FOR TEENS
PUBLISHED BY WATERBROOK PRESS
2375 Telstar Drive, Suite 160
Colorado Springs, Colorado 80920
A division of Random House, Inc.

ISBN 1-57856-731-9

Printed in Canada
2004—First Edition

10 9 8 7 6 5 4 3 2 1

Since this book is designed to help parents encourage their teenagers, we want to dedicate it in loving gratitude to our parents—the late Henry Curtis McDaniel Sr., Velma R. "Babs" McDaniel, the late Abraham David Preston, and Joan W. Preston—for our godly upbringing and for their loving parental influence. We have a rich heritage to pass on to our own teens, Curtis McDaniel III, Megan McDaniel, and Heather McDaniel. May God, our great Savior, receive the glory as parents use this book to encourage their teens. And may homes be strengthened in the fear and nurture of the Lord Jesus.

ACKNOWLEDGMENTS

Special thanks go to the following:

To our children—Curtis, Megan, and Heather—for reading and field-testing most, if not all, of these devotions in their school life.

To our many family members, friends, and faithful prayer partners in Virginia; the St. Louis area; Montgomery, Alabama; Middle Tennessee; southern Kentucky; Fort Lauderdale, Florida; and Butler, Pennsylvania, for their faithful intercession for this work.

To these and others we offer our heartfelt thanks for help, encouragement, and prayers.

Your Teens Need Your Encouragement

The world is a daily battleground for the souls of our teenagers. When our sons and daughters are with friends, at school, at work, or practicing sports, they often find themselves in an environment that is hostile to the values we uphold as Christian families. How can parents influence and encourage their teens at the times they need it the most—when the pressures of peers and the power of ungodly influences seek to pull them down?

Many youth want to live for Christ when they're at school. However, they dread the possibility of being jeered by antagonistic students. How can we encourage them to keep their eyes fixed upon Jesus during the school day and when they're with friends? How can we help provide an added injection of Christian truth to get them through a tough day?

Life Brighteners for Teens equips parents to encourage their junior high and senior high children to take the Word of God with them. The ninety verses of Scripture, with related "life brightener" thoughts, enable parents to bring biblical truth to light to encourage the hearts of their teenagers.

How to Use Life Brighteners

This book is organized under thirty topics, representing life issues that your teenager encounters regularly. Each topic has three pertinent verses of Scripture with related Life Brightener messages. The back of each page gives you an opportunity to write a personal note to your teen. Then simply fold the page and insert it into your teenager's backpack or lunch bag. Sending your teen off with a personal Life Brightener will take only seconds, but the impact will last all day long!

Each day's Life Brightener gives you the opportunity to touch your teen's life with God's truth. Every day, or as often as you choose, you can:

- Give your teen a biblical pick-me-up for the day.
- Communicate your care while you and your teen are apart.
- Arm your teenagers with biblical truth to encourage and strengthen them.
- Lead your teen to see the beauty and adventure of a personal relationship with Jesus Christ.
- Motivate your teenager to apply Scripture by offering practical suggestions for living out God's truth.
- Equip your teen to be an effective witness to others.

As you use the encouraging messages in this book, pray for your teenagers. Ask the Holy Spirit to use the Word of God to mold their lives for Christ.

God's Eyes

The eyes of the LORD are everywhere,
keeping watch on the wicked and the good.

PROVERBS 15:3

Today's Life Brightener

No matter where you go, God is already there. He knows everything about you. What does he see in your life today?

Special Notes:

●--●

●--●

●--●

●--●

Hang On!

Blessed is the man who perseveres under trial....

JAMES 1:12

Today's Life Brightener

You're probably facing some sort of "trial"—maybe taking tests! God blesses us when we keep on going. So give it your best, and trust God with whatever happens.

Special Notes:

The Right Time

There is a time for everything,
and a season for every activity under heaven.

ECCLESIASTES 3:1

Today's Life Brightener

There's a time set aside for different things in life. When you're a student, it's the time for taking tests. Just do your best to honor the Lord. Good grades or not, I love you!

Special Notes:

How's Your Heart?

...God does not judge by external appearance....

GALATIANS 2:6

Today's Life Brightener

Some people judge us based on what we look like. But that's not what gets God's attention. He's concerned about your heart, not your hairstyle.

Special Notes:

●- ●

●- ●

●- ●

●- ●

You're Valuable!

There is neither Jew nor Greek, slave nor free, male nor female,

for you are all one in Christ Jesus.

GALATIANS 3:28

Today's Life Brightener

People make assumptions based on a person's skin color, gender, or clothes. But God sees you in a completely different light. In God's eyes, you're incredibly valuable!

Special Notes:

Real Beauty

Your beauty should...be that of your inner self,
the unfading beauty of a gentle and quiet spirit....

1 PETER 3:3-4

Today's Life Brightener

Don't you get tired of movies and television shows that glorify the beautiful people? It's enough to give you a headache. God's concerned about your inner life. How are things inside you today?

Special Notes:

Need Some Refreshment?

...he who refreshes others will himself be refreshed.

PROVERBS 11:25

Today's Life Brightener

The Bible is often upside down. For instance, if you help somebody else, you'll find spiritual refreshment. Look around. Who needs a good word?

Special Notes:

Helping Somebody

...whoever is kind to the needy honors God.

PROVERBS 14:31

Today's Life Brightener

Everybody's needy, whether they're rich or poor. Did a friend forget to bring a lunch? Does someone need help with homework? I love it when you find ways to help others!

Special Notes:

● -- ●

● -- ●

● -- ●

● -- ●

Golden Words

A word aptly spoken is like apples of gold in settings of silver.

PROVERBS 25:11

Today's Life Brightener

"A word aptly spoken" means you say the right thing at the right time, and it lifts someone's spirit. Think about who needs this the most, and then go for it!

Special Notes:

Real Change

Therefore, if anyone is in Christ, he is a new creation....

2 CORINTHIANS 5:17

Today's Life Brightener

When Jesus saved you, he made you a new person. Your attitudes, priorities, and interests were made different from the world's. Do the people around you notice a change?

Special Notes:

Finally, the Truth

...The body is not meant for sexual immorality, but for the Lord,
and the Lord for the body.

1 CORINTHIANS 6:13

Today's Life Brightener

God created your body for the Holy Spirit's residence, giving you the greatest satisfaction ever. There's nothing more important than offering your body to God. Let him be your Leader!

Special Notes:

Real Satisfaction

...I am the bread of life. He who comes to me will never go hungry,
and he who believes in me will never be thirsty.

JOHN 6:35

Today's Life Brightener

During lunch today, give this some thought: Jesus satisfies us as nothing else ever will. What does that mean to you?

Special Notes:

●------------------------------------●

●------------------------------------●

●------------------------------------●

●------------------------------------●

Take a Stand

Blessed are those who are persecuted because of righteousness,

for theirs is the kingdom of heaven.

MATTHEW 5:10

Today's Life Brightener

If people attack you verbally or even physically because you're witnessing for Jesus, he says you're blessed for it. God honors people who stand up for him. Where are you standing?

Special Notes:

Feeling Insulted?

Blessed are you when people insult you...because of me.

MATTHEW 5:11

Today's Life Brightener

No one likes to be mocked. Jesus endured the worst insults, even though he lived a perfect life. The next time someone ridicules you, remember: Jesus understands perfectly.

Special Notes:

Don't Back Down

You too, be patient and stand firm, because the Lord's coming is near.

JAMES 5:8

Today's Life Brightener

The same power of God that raised Jesus from the dead is at work in your life. You have everything you need to stand firm!

Special Notes:

●---●

●---●

●---●

●---●

God's Favor

...Let the light of your face shine upon us, O LORD.

PSALM 4:6

Today's Life Brightener

The shepherd boy who became Israel's greatest king wisely asked for God's favor. If you ask with humility, God will honor you. He wants his glory and favor to shine on you!

Special Notes:

Don't Give In

Therefore, my dear brothers, stand firm. Let nothing move you....

1 CORINTHIANS 15:58

Today's Life Brightener

When your spiritual roots are deep in Christ and his Word, you'll be strong enough to resist temptation. Don't give in to Satan's distractions. Remember, God is backing you up!

Special Notes:

God's Rewards

You need to persevere so that when you have done the will of God,

you will receive what he has promised.

HEBREWS 10:36

Today's Life Brightener

God owns everything, and he gives big rewards. But you have to do your part. Whatever you're doing, give it everything you've got.

Special Notes:

Feeling Hurt?

The LORD is close to the brokenhearted
and saves those who are crushed in spirit.

PSALM 34:18

Today's Life Brightener

Even close friends can hurt you. It's not fair, but it's life. If you're feeling used and tossed aside, remember that God specializes in healing broken hearts.

Special Notes:

• -- •

• -- •

• -- •

• -- •

Great Medicine

A cheerful heart is good medicine....

PROVERBS 17:22

Today's Life Brightener

Feeling down? The best medicine is found in your heart. Do something that makes you happy—call a friend or get some exercise. Whatever helps, just do it!

Special Notes:

Down and Up

Why are you downcast, O my soul?...

Put your hope in God,

for I will yet praise him....

PSALM 42:5

Today's Life Brightener

If you're going through a down time, remember that God is there for you every day. So remember to look up!

Special Notes:

How's Your Spirit?

Blessed are the poor in spirit,

for theirs is the kingdom of heaven.

MATTHEW 5:3

Today's Life Brightener

Being poor in spirit has nothing to do with possessions or feeling sad. It means that you realize your spiritual life is miserable apart from God. But with God, you're blessed!

Special Notes:

When God Moves In

Don't you know that you yourselves are God's temple
and that God's Spirit lives in you?

1 CORINTHIANS 3:16

Today's Life Brightener

You are a unique, special-production person. God made you who you are so his Spirit can move in. Do you need to clear out some room for him?

Special Notes:

It's All God

May I never boast except in the cross of our Lord Jesus Christ....

GALATIANS 6:14

Today's Life Brightener

God loved us so much that he sent Christ to die for us. That's the most humbling truth any of us can imagine. God did it all, and there's nothing we can add.

Special Notes:

Look Around

Be on your guard....

1 CORINTHIANS 16:13

Today's Life Brightener

There's a lot going on, and it's not all good. God tells us to be aware of what's happening around us. So watch for God's work while you're watching out for the activities of the devil.

Special Notes:

No Matter What

But the fruit of the Spirit is…faithfulness.

GALATIANS 5:22

Today's Life Brightener

A lot of people lose interest quickly and just quit, but God wants us in it for the long haul. He wants followers who will stay with him no matter what happens.

Special Notes:

Keep Trying!

Let us not become weary in doing good,
for at the proper time we will reap a harvest if we do not give up.

GALATIANS 6:9

Today's Life Brightener

Coaches drill it into their players: don't give up. Keep working, preparing, trying. The same thing applies in life. No matter how difficult the work, stay with it!

Special Notes:

●---●

●---●

●---●

●---●

Real Friends

Blessed is the man

who does not walk in the counsel of the wicked

...or sit in the seat of mockers.

PSALM 1:1

Today's Life Brightener

You know how important it is to have a friend who stands with you no matter what others are doing. Pick your friends carefully. A true friend is a real gift!

Special Notes:

Wasted Time

But avoid foolish controversies…and arguments and quarrels
about the law, because these are unprofitable and useless.

TITUS 3:9

Today's Life Brightener

You know people who make a big deal out of nothing. They're always look-ing for something to get worked up about. Don't take the bait. They're just wasting your time.

Special Notes:

Heart Protection

Above all else, guard your heart,
for it is the wellspring of life.
PROVERBS 4:23

Today's Life Brightener

There's plenty of spiritual pollution out there. So watch where you go, what you read and watch, and who you spend time with. I love you, so be careful!

Special Notes:

Something to Give

...they opened their treasures and presented him
with gifts of gold and of incense and of myrrh.

MATTHEW 2:11

Today's Life Brightener

The wise men worshiped Jesus by giving him meaningful gifts. Of all the presents you will give to others this year, what will you give to Jesus?

Special Notes:

Want a Blessing?

A generous man will himself be blessed,

for he shares his food with the poor.

PROVERBS 22:9

Today's Life Brightener

Looking for a huge blessing? Give something away! Give someone your time or your attention or a listening ear. God will give you something awesome in return.

Special Notes:

Real Treasure

Command them...to be generous and willing to share.
In this way they will lay up treasure
for themselves...for the coming age....

1 TIMOTHY 6:18-19

Today's Life Brightener

There is great reward today in being generous, but some rewards are waiting for you in heaven. Look around and see who needs your generosity.

Special Notes:

When to Be Thankful

[G]ive thanks in all circumstances....

1 THESSALONIANS 5:18

Today's Life Brightener

Is it tough to be thankful today? Is a classmate getting on your nerves? Is there a teacher who's really hard to get along with? Start giving God thanks now and see what happens.

Special Notes:

God's Gifts

And whatever you do...do it all in the name of the Lord Jesus,
giving thanks to God the Father through him.

COLOSSIANS 3:17

Today's Life Brightener

Even the everyday things in life come from God. Thank him for all his gifts, like good food, good friends, and a family that loves you. I'm thankful for you!

Special Notes:

God's Care

It is because of him that you are in Christ Jesus....
1 CORINTHIANS 1:30

Today's Life Brightener

Long before you were born, God was thinking about you. He continues to love you and to care for you every day. It's part of his job description, designed for your benefit!

Special Notes:

Stay on Your Toes

Let no one deceive you with empty words....

EPHESIANS 5:6

Today's Life Brightener

Satan can make almost anything look really good, but in God's presence the same thing is empty and meaningless. Satan wants to distract you, so ask God to keep you alert!

Special Notes:

Divine Directions

Trust in the LORD with all your heart....

PROVERBS 3:5

Today's Life Brightener

Since God knows everything, he is the natural Person to ask for directions. But remember that his guidance isn't always "logical." Can you still trust him?

Special Notes:

- --
- --
- --
- --

Great Advice

...keep your father's commands
and do not forsake your mother's teaching....
When you walk, they will guide you....

PROVERBS 6:20,22

Today's Life Brightener

When you pay attention to godly wisdom, God uses it to lead you in the right direction. Follow God's Word and listen to your parents' advice. That's successful living!

Special Notes:

How to Win

But thanks be to God! He gives us the victory

through our Lord Jesus Christ.

1 CORINTHIANS 15:57

Today's Life Brightener

Because of Jesus, you have great hope in life! Do your friends see his victory in you?

Special Notes:

Real Life

Now this is eternal life: that they may know you....

JOHN 17:3

Today's Life Brightener

The only way you can know your Father in heaven is through knowing Christ. That kind of relationship brings hope!

Special Notes:

The Best News

...God has given us eternal life, and this life is in his Son.

1 JOHN 5:11

Today's Life Brightener

God's best news is that we have eternal life through the gift of his Son. Let that promise from God lighten your load and ease your concerns today.

Special Notes:

Better Directions

He guides the humble in what is right

and teaches them his way.

PSALM 25:9

Today's Life Brightener

God knows what's best for you, and he wants to guide you in the right direction today and always. I'm glad you want to listen to him!

Special Notes:

What's Important?

Humble yourselves before the Lord,

and he will lift you up.

JAMES 4:10

Today's Life Brightener

If you try to make yourself seem important, you're guaranteed to fail. But if you want to please God, start helping people. Who could use some help today?

Special Notes:

Who Goes First?

The fear of the LORD teaches a man wisdom,
and humility comes before honor.

PROVERBS 15:33

Today's Life Brightener

If you serve others, you'll be honored in return. God notices when you put others ahead of yourself. That sort of thing is important to him!

Special Notes:

---•

---•

---•

---•

Divine Joy

Be joyful always.

1 THESSALONIANS 5:16

Today's Life Brightener

Maybe a good friend is moving away, or you forgot to turn in an important assignment. If you're having a down day, stick close to Jesus. His joy comes through even when life stinks.

Special Notes:

Real Strength

> ...Do not grieve, for the joy of the LORD is your strength.
>
> NEHEMIAH 8:10

Today's Life Brightener

Are you hurting? You need a joy encounter. Ask God to strengthen your heart with his joy.

Special Notes:

Passionate Joy

I have no greater joy than to hear
that my children are walking in the truth.

3 JOHN 4

Today's Life Brightener

The greatest joy you can bring to God is your growing passion for his Word and your desire to obey him. I'm glad you want to follow him!

Special Notes:

The Best Work

Whatever you do, work at it with all your heart....
COLOSSIANS 3:23

Today's Life Brightener

Right now your primary work and calling are your studies. Put your heart into your schoolwork. God is glorified when you do your best!

Special Notes:

Things That Last

...your labor in the Lord is not in vain.

1 CORINTHIANS 15:58

Today's Life Brightener

Don't get discouraged if you're devoting yourself to God but aren't seeing visible results. Stay true to God, and leave the results up to him. He knows your heart!

Special Notes:

Lessons Learned

Hold on to instruction, do not let it go....

PROVERBS 4:13

Today's Life Brightener

It's easy to forget the important things—lessons about character, faithfulness, discipline, honesty, and dedication. This kind of "instruction" is always in style.

Special Notes:

A Real Friend

...And surely I am with you always, to the very end of the age.

MATTHEW 28:20

Today's Life Brightener

You may feel alone, but no matter what's happening, God is with you. While some people might ignore you, Jesus promises to be your closest friend!

Special Notes:

A Constant Friend

...God has said,
"Never will I leave you;
never will I forsake you."

HEBREWS 13:5

Today's Life Brightener

No matter how other people treat you, remember that Jesus is there to pick you back up. He's a Friend you can depend on!

Special Notes:

God Remembers

He has remembered his love
and his faithfulness....
PSALM 98:3

Today's Life Brightener

When people ignore you and you begin to wonder if anyone cares about you, think about this: God remembers you. He loves you too much to ever let you down!

Special Notes:

The Best Investment

[F]or riches do not endure forever....

PROVERBS 27:24

Today's Life Brightener

The world cares way too much about money and things like designer clothes, cars, and trips. God says those things don't last. But all of God's things will last forever!

Special Notes:

How Much Is Enough?

Whoever loves money never has money enough....

ECCLESIASTES 5:10

Today's Life Brightener

Be careful what you become attached to. The Bible says if you chase money and possessions, you'll never get any rest. Are you happy with what you have?

Special Notes:

A Great Money Habit

...Some people, eager for money, have wandered from the faith....
1 TIMOTHY 6:10

Today's Life Brightener

Jesus wants us to love him more than money. Give this a try: save 10 percent of what you earn, give at least 10 percent to God, and use what remains for personal expenses. See what happens!

Special Notes:

Getting What You Need

Finally, be strong in the Lord and in his mighty power.

EPHESIANS 6:10

Today's Life Brightener

God is all-powerful, and he is eager to give you everything you need for today. I hope you'll tell him what you need.

Special Notes:

●--●

●--●

●--●

●--●

Ask for Something Big

And my God will meet all your needs
according to his glorious riches in Christ Jesus.
PHILIPPIANS 4:19

Today's Life Brightener

With God there are no shortages. Do you need patience, courage, peace of mind, comfort? God has plenty of all those things. Just ask!

Special Notes:

Get Ready to Receive

For the LORD God is a sun and shield;...

no good thing does he withhold

from those whose walk is blameless.

PSALM 84:11

Today's Life Brightener

God wants to bless you in amazing ways! But first your life must be right before him. Ask for his forgiveness, then see what he'll do for you.

Special Notes:

Real Peace

...and the LORD has laid on him the iniquity of us all.

ISAIAH 53:6

Today's Life Brightener

Because Jesus bore your sin and guilt, you don't have to carry it around anymore! God wants to lighten your load. You can accept his forgiveness and enjoy his peace. Are you ready?

Special Notes:

Eternal Certainty

I write these things to you who believe in the name of the Son of God

so that you may know that you have eternal life.

1 JOHN 5:13

Today's Life Brightener

You don't have to wonder whether you're going to heaven when you die.
God says you can know for sure. There's no need for doubt!

Special Notes:

Waging Peace

But the fruit of the Spirit is…peace….

GALATIANS 5:22

Today's Life Brightener

Sadly, there's always a war going on somewhere. And every news report talks about violent crime. But if you know Christ, you have God's peace. Do you have his peace today?

Special Notes:

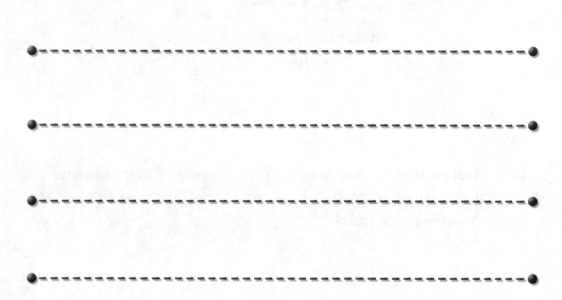

Win the Battle

Do not be overcome by evil, but overcome evil with good.

ROMANS 12:21

Today's Life Brightener

Sometimes people will make fun of you and your beliefs. But don't get discouraged. Instead, be kind to them, just like Jesus treated those who doubted him. Maybe they'll change their minds!

Special Notes:

Need Courage?

...stand firm in the faith; be men of courage; be strong.

1 CORINTHIANS 16:13

Today's Life Brightener

It's easy to quit when things turn against you. It takes a lot more courage to hang in there. So don't give up. Just start asking God for courage!

Special Notes:

●--●

●--●

●--●

●--●

The Finish Line

You need to persevere so that when you have done the will of God,

you will receive what he has promised.

HEBREWS 10:36

Today's Life Brightener

A school year is a lot like a marathon: it takes everything you've got to finish. God will give you strength, so don't stop now! Keep running to the end, and cross the finish line with God.

Special Notes:

Expect the Unexpected

...be prepared in season and out of season....
2 TIMOTHY 4:2

Today's Life Brightener

Life throws us a lot of curves, so prepare for surprises. Expect interruptions, delays, and schedule changes. A little planning now will save you time and frustration later on.

Special Notes:

Plan for the Best

But the noble man makes noble plans,
and by noble deeds he stands.
ISAIAH 32:8

Today's Life Brightener

Are you careful to get in enough study, rest, and time for fun? God wants you to organize your day so you can enjoy the best things. It only takes a few minutes, and it's worth it!

Special Notes:

Why Get Organized?

But everything should be done in a fitting and orderly way.

1 CORINTHIANS 14:40

Today's Life Brightener

Think about the structure of a molecule or the path of the planets. God had to be organized to create the universe out of nothing. It may not sound exciting, but getting organized makes a big difference!

Special Notes:

Getting Started

Lazy hands make a man poor,
but diligent hands bring wealth.
PROVERBS 10:4

Today's Life Brightener

Is there a big project you've been putting off? Remember, the best way to get finished is to get started. Stick with it. Then you can relax when it's over.

Special Notes:

What Are You Waiting For?

Do not boast about tomorrow,

for you do not know what a day may bring forth.

PROVERBS 27:1

Today's Life Brightener

If you have something important to do, it's smart to get it done today. That way, the most important things get your best effort—and tomorrow you'll have time for yourself.

Special Notes:

Work You'll Enjoy

Again you will plant vineyards...

the farmers will plant them and enjoy their fruit.

JEREMIAH 31:5

Today's Life Brightener

Farmers plant crops in the spring to produce food in the fall. If they started putting things off, we'd all get pretty hungry. You're working hard today. Look forward to enjoying the results!

Special Notes:

It's God Calling

...I stand at the door and knock. If anyone hears my voice
and opens the door, I will come in....

REVELATION 3:20

Today's Life Brightener

Jesus doesn't force his way into our lives, but he does invite us to open
the door to him. God gently knocks at your heart. Will you let him in?

Special Notes:

Visible Change

...Jesus declared, "I tell you the truth, no one can see
the kingdom of God unless he is born again."

JOHN 3:3

Today's Life Brightener

Being born again is a spiritual act where God changes your life from the inside out. Does your life show others that you're born again? A changed life is a powerful message.

Special Notes:

Spiritual Sickness

...It is not the healthy who need a doctor, but the sick.

LUKE 5:31

Today's Life Brightener

Sin is a spiritual sickness, and Jesus is the only one who can heal it. If we recognize our sickness and admit we need his healing, Jesus saves us. How's your spiritual condition?

Special Notes:

●------------------------------------●

●------------------------------------●

●------------------------------------●

●------------------------------------●

God Doesn't Quit

...he who began a good work in you

will carry it on to completion until the day of Christ Jesus.

PHILIPPIANS 1:6

Today's Life Brightener

God has started working in your life, and he isn't going to quit now. I love seeing the results of what he is doing in you!

Special Notes:

God Is Up Close

Know that the LORD has set apart the godly for himself....

PSALM 4:3

Today's Life Brightener

You're somebody special! That's why God wants a closer relationship with you than you can imagine. Are you letting him come close?

Special Notes:

Call Him "Daddy"

Because you are sons, God sent the Spirit of his Son into our hearts,

the Spirit who calls out, "Abba, Father."

GALATIANS 4:6

Today's Life Brightener

Being a Christian is a daily relationship with God, the Creator of the universe. And he wants you to call him "Daddy." (That's what Abba means.) Wow!

Special Notes:

God's Formula for Success

But his delight is in the law of the LORD,

and on his law he meditates day and night....

Whatever he does prospers.

PSALM 1:2-3

Today's Life Brightener

Want success? Stay away from the wrong people, read the Bible every day, meditate on God's words, and stay grounded in his grace. With that, you'll move forward in success God's way.

Special Notes:

Step Aside

Commit to the LORD whatever you do,

and your plans will succeed.

PROVERBS 16:3

Today's Life Brightener

When you really want God to be in the center of your life, you step aside and make room. Then he puts himself and his plans in your life. God won't direct your life until you let go.

Special Notes:

Success Through Service

...serve one another in love.

GALATIANS 5:13

Today's Life Brightener

Jesus set the example: we're here to serve others. It was his mission on earth, and it's what he expects from us. I'm glad you look for ways to serve others!

Special Notes:

Jesus Helps

No temptation has seized you except what is common to man....
1 CORINTHIANS 10:13

Today's Life Brightener

If you're struggling right now, be encouraged that your temptations are the same ones other people face. In fact, Jesus knows exactly what you're going through, so get his help!

Special Notes:

Strength Training

...And God is faithful; he will not let you be tempted
beyond what you can bear....

1 CORINTHIANS 10:13

Today's Life Brightener

God allows certain temptations into your life so he can build your
character during the tough times. It's hard, but it's also really good
news. God is making you a stronger person!

Special Notes:

God's Escape Hatch

...But when you are tempted, he will also provide a way out

so that you can stand up under it.

1 CORINTHIANS 10:13

Today's Life Brightener

When temptation threatens to overpower you, look for God's escape hatch. He promises that it's always there!

Special Notes:

The Best Opportunities

Teach us to number our days aright,

that we may gain a heart of wisdom.

PSALM 90:12

Today's Life Brightener

If you don't take advantage of opportunities now, you might never get the chance again. How can you make the best use of the days God is giving you?

Special Notes:

_____

_____

_____

_____

Life's Priorities

What I mean, brothers, is that the time is short....

1 CORINTHIANS 7:29

Today's Life Brightener

When Jesus returned to heaven, he promised that he would come back to earth again. That means the time might be short. What are you doing today to make your life really count?

Special Notes:

●- ●

●- ●

●- ●

●- ●

Get Started!

As long as it is day, we must do the work of him who sent me.

Night is coming, when no one can work.

JOHN 9:4

Today's Life Brightener

Go ahead and get started doing the most important things now. Since your time is limited, use it wisely!

Special Notes:

Breathing Praise

Let everything that has breath praise the LORD....

PSALM 150:6

Today's Life Brightener

You were created to praise God in everything you do—even in breathing! Praising God with your entire being makes him happy. Think about that as you go through your day.

Special Notes:

- ---
- ---
- ---
- ---

Tell God "Thanks"

O LORD, our Lord,
how majestic is your name in all the earth!...
PSALM 8:1

Today's Life Brightener

You've made it through another day full of hassles and frustration. So praise God for getting you through it. Take a minute to tell him thanks for the great things he's done for you lately.

Special Notes:

●---●

●---●

●---●

●---●

The Best Help

Christ redeemed us from the curse of the law....

GALATIANS 3:13

Today's Life Brightener

You can't obey all of God's laws on your own, no matter how hard you try. So praise God for his Spirit, who helps you live in obedience. You couldn't do it without him.

Special Notes:

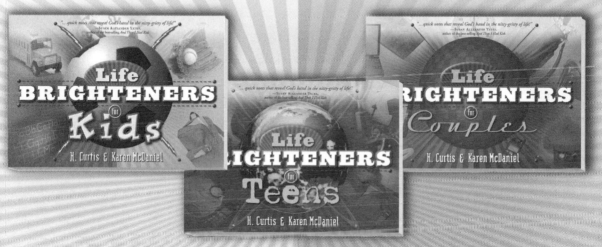